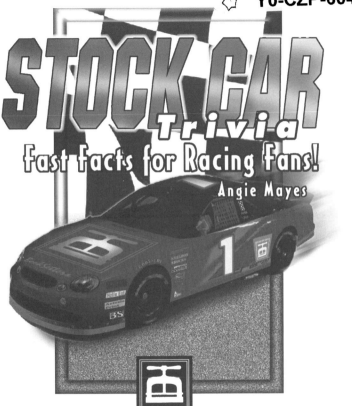

STOCK CAR

Trivia

Fast Facts for Racing Fans!

Angie Mayes

PREMIUM PRESS AMERICA
NASHVILLE, TENNESSEE

Stock Car Trivia: Fast Facts for Racing Fans!

© 1999 by PREMIUM PRESS AMERICA

ISBN 1-887654-72-0

Library of Congress Catalog Card Number 99-70379

PREMIUM PRESS AMERICA books are available at special discounts for premiums, sales promotions, fund-raising, or educational use. For details contact the Publisher at P.O. Box 159015, Nashville, TN 37215; or phone 800-891-7323.

Come visit our web site at www.premiumpress.com.

Cover and interior design by Bob Bubnis/BookSetters—bksetters@aol.com
Edited by Mardy Fones

Printed by Vaughan Printing

First Printing May 1999
1 2 3 4 5 6 7 8 9 10

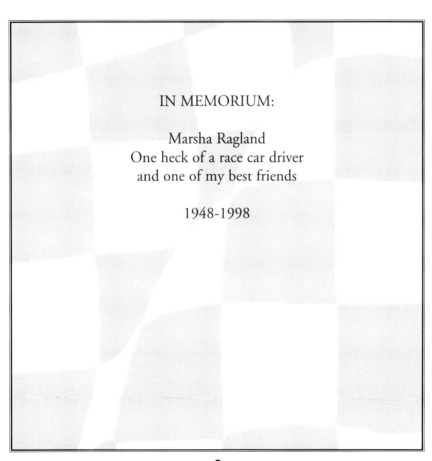

IN MEMORIUM:

Marsha Ragland
One heck of a race car driver
and one of my best friends

1948-1998

Table of Contents

NASCAR AND MUSIC CITY -1

SUPER SPEEDWAYS -13

DAYTONA 500 -17

WINNING -21

THE WINSTON -25

NASCAR AND THE FANS - - - - - - - - - - - - - - - - - - -29

CREW CHIEFS -33

TRACKS -37

ROOKIES -41

STOCK CAR TRIVIA

RECORDS -45

SECOND GENERATION DRIVERS - - - - - - - - - - - - - - -49

SCHOOLS -51

NICKNAMES -55

EARLY RACING HISTORY - - - - - - - - - - - - - - - - - -57

BUSCH GRAND NATIONAL - - - - - - - - - - - - - - - -61

SPONSORS -65

BUD SHOOTOUT -69

TRUE OR FALSE -73

HOBBIES -77

STOCK CAR TRIVIA

COOL FACTS -81

CAR OWNERS -85

MONEY AND OTHER IMPORTANT NUMBERS - - - - - - - - - -89

FIRST AND LAST -93

WRECKS -97

CRAFTSMAN TRUCK SERIES - - - - - - - - - - - - - - - -101

DRIVERS -105

MORE DRIVERS -109

TRUE OR FALSE, PART TWO - - - - - - - - - - - - - - - -113

PART-TIME JOBS -117

STOCK CAR TRIVIA

THE LEGENDS -121

HOW TO ORDER -125

NASCAR AND MUSIC CITY

1. Name the first racing-related country music album.

2. Columbia Records produced two NASCAR albums. One was "Hotter Than Asphalt." Name the other.

3. This country artist competed in 43 Grand National races in the '60s and '70s.

4. A protegé of Bobby Hamilton, this Nashville racer began racing go-karts before he was 10 and captured a National Karting Championship when he was 13.

5. Geoff Bodine and Darrell Waltrip sang on a country album. True or False?

6. Which country artist sang the theme for the stock car movie "Stroker Ace"?

7. Whose salsa company was a sponsor on Geoff Bodine's car?

8. This former president of Nashville Speedway USA was a founder of the NASCAR All-Pro series.

9. Which country group's song and video were called "Richard Petty Fans"?

10. Winston Cup cars used to visit what is now Nashville Speedway USA. True or False?

11. Which country duo hosted a Legends Car Series in Nashville each Summer?

12. Which current driver "dabbled" in country music?

13. Kyle Petty sang a song about his dad entitled
    _____.

14. This Nashville-based network features quite a bit of stock car racing.

15. Which record company executive owned Richard Petty's race car in '84?

NASCAR AND MUSIC CITY
ANSWERS

1. "NASCAR Goes Country"
2. "Running Wide Open."
3. Marty Robbins
4. Casey Atwood
5. True
6. Charlie Daniels
7. Tanya Tucker
8. Bob Harmon
9. Alabama
10. True
11. Brooks & Dunn
12. Kyle Petty
13. "Oh, King Richard"
14. TNN (The Nashville Network)
15. Mike Curb of Curb Records

SUPERSPEEDWAYS

1. All of this driver's wins at Michigan were back to back.

2. This driver left his car mid-race at the Talladega 500 in '73 because "something" told him to quit.

3. True or false. Atlanta Motor Speedway was built in '74.

4. This 44-acre lake has been the resting place for many drivers at Daytona International Speedway, including Goody's Dash Series driver Dave Stacy.

5. Which track saw the closest 1-2-3 race in history?

6. What was the first pace car at Daytona in '59?

7. Who established the world's closed course speed record (221.120 m.p.h.) at Talladega in '75?

8. Roger Penske owns two super-speedways. Name them.

9. Which track saw the final championship battle between Alan Kulwicki and Davey Allison, the first Cup race for Jeff Gordon and the final race for Richard Petty? For a bonus, what was the year?

10. Who is the oldest driver to win a race on a super-speedway?

11. This track was the site of the first major victory by third-generation driver, Dale Earnhardt Jr.

12. Which "modern day" driver has the most super-speedway wins (44)?

13. Riverside International Speedway was the site of this driver's first Winston Cup win. True or False?

14. This tri-oval track in Pennsylvania measures 2.5 miles. True or False?

15. Which driver has won the most superspeedway races?

SUPERSPEEDWAY
ANSWERS

1. Cale Yarborough
2. Bobby Isaac
3. False, '60
4. Lake Lloyd
5. Talladega
6. Bonneville Convertible
7. Mark Donohue
8. Michigan and California
9. Atlanta, '92
10. Harry Gant ('92   52 years old)
11. Texas Motor Speedway
12. David Pearson ('72-'86)
13. Tim Richmond
14. Pocono
15. Richard Petty ('58-'92)

DAYTONA 500

1. Jeff Gordon is the only driver to win the Daytona 500 and the _____ in the same year.

2. Which drivers won the Daytona 500 back to back?

3. Name the years that Richard Petty won this honor back to back.

4. The Daytona 500 trophy is also known as the _____ trophy.

5. For the second time in his career, _____ held off Dale Earnhardt for the Daytona 500 win in '96.

STOCK CAR TRIVIA

6. The winner of the '63 Daytona 500 was

   _____.

7. What Winston Cup driver won the race with a checkerboard design on his car?

8. Who won the Daytona 500 four times ('68, '77, '83, '84)?

9. What current driver holds the Daytona 500 qualifying record?

10. Which regular Indy-car drivers also won the Daytona 500?

11. Who won the first Daytona 500?

12. This driver won his first Daytona 500 event in '98.

13. Which driver was the only one to win a "triple" award at Daytona (three races during speed weeks)?

14. He was the first to win the Daytona 500 and the Firecracker 250 in the same year.

15. Which two men, sharing the same last name, won the '68 and '69 Daytona 500 races, respectively?

DAYTONA 500
ANSWERS

1. Winston Cup Championship
2. Cale Yarborough, Richard Petty and Sterling Marlin
3. '73 and '74
4. Harley J. Earl
5. Dale Jarrett
6. Tiny Lund
7. Derrick Cope in a Puralator car
8. Cale Yarborough
9. Bill Elliot (210.364 m.p.h.)
10. Mario Andretti ('67) and A.J. Foyt ('72)
11. Lee Petty
12. Dale Earnhardt
13. Cale Yarborough
14. Fireball Roberts ('62)
15. Cale ('68) and Lee Roy ('69) Yarborough

WINNING

1. He has won a race every year since he started in '83.

2. In '96, Bobby Hamilton brought a Petty Enterprises-owned car to victory lane for the first time since what year?

3. In Richard Petty's last two wins (#199, #200) in '84, the car was owned by whom?

4. The late Elmo Langley ended his NASCAR racing career in _____, nearly 15 years after winning his first and second (and only) races.

5. To win the Winston Million, a driver has to win what races and at what tracks?

6. What uncredited driver led an actual race at Phoenix International Raceway in a Rick Hendrick Research and Development (R&D) car in the movie "Days of Thunder"?

7. These brothers won at the same time, during the same race: one took the race win, one took the championship. Also, name the track and the year.

8. No defending champion of the Winston Select 500 has repeated as the winner since _____ in '75 and '76, breaking David Pearson's string of three wins, '72-'74.

9. With Andy Petree as his crew chief, _____ took a stunning win at Talladega in '88.

10. Who was the youngest driver to ever win a race?

11. Name the modern day drivers with the most wins in a season. How many wins?

12. Lee Petty had whose victory reversed at Lakewood Speedway?

13. This car owner had the top three cars at the finish of the '97 Daytona 500.

14. Who won the last race at Riverside International Speedway?

15. Which set of brothers has four wins two each in '95?

WINNING
ANSWERS

1. Ricky Rudd
2. '83
3. Mike Curb
4. '66
5. Daytona 500, Daytona; Winston Select 500, Talladega; Coca Cola 600, Charlotte; Southern 500, Darlington
6. Bobby Hamilton
7. Bobby Labonte took the win in the Napa 500 while brother Terry won the Winston Cup Championship. The track was Atlanta Motor Speedway and the year was '97.
8. Buddy Baker
9. Phil Parsons
10. Donald Thomas
11. Richard Petty and Jeff Gordon. Petty won 13 in '75, while Gordon won 13 in '98
12. Richard Petty, Lee was named the winner
13. Rick Hendrick. Jeff Gordon, Terry Labonte and Ricky Craven took the top three spots
14. Rusty Wallace
15. Terry and Bobby Labonte

THE WINSTON

1. Which younger brother of a former Winston Cup champion staged a major upset at the '96 Winston?

2. Who won the first Winston?

3. The Winston is the richest race per _____ in all of motorsports.

4. The race was to be run on various tracks, the second being _____. They now hold the race at Charlotte each year.

5. The race is sponsored by

   _____

6. Bill Elliot won The Winston on which current track?

STOCK CAR TRIVIA

7. To get into the Winston, a driver must have won races in the _____ years?

8. The race is run in _____ segments.

9. Who won each of the segments in '95?

10. The first Winston was held in what year?

11. There are special entrance exceptions: one for a champion who is still an active driver and another for the past five winners of the _____.

12. The winner of the Winston Open is not guaranteed a spot in the Winston Select. True or False?

13. All Winston Cup competitors are invited to compete in the Winston Open. True or False?

14. Dale Earnhardt changed his car color to
_____ in '95 to commemorate R.J.
Reynolds' 25th anniversary.

15. The Winston Select has at least _____ cars
in the field.

THE WINSTON
ANSWERS

1. Michael Waltrip
2. Darrell Waltrip
3. Mile
4. Atlanta
5. R.J. Reynolds
6. Atlanta
7. Preceding and current
8. Three
9. Jeff Gordon
10. '85
11. Winston Select
12. False
13. True
14. Silver
15. 20

NASCAR AND THE FANS

1. NASCAR has a chain of theme stores called what?

2. The official fan club of NASCAR is called what?

3. An interactive mini-theme park at Daytona is called what?

4. _____ is just one of many restaurants with stock car themes. The first one opened in Myrtle Beach.

5. NASCAR has an online address. True or False?

6. Richard Petty's Fan Apprecaition Tour took place in what year?

7. Each year the fans vote on an award given at the Winston Cup awards banquet. What is it called?

8. Which driver has been voted a fan favorite more than any other?

9. Who broke Elliot's string of wins?

10. Which car manufacturer has made more than 1 billion cars and made a special doll for the sport?

11. When the race was stopped early because the track's surface "came up," nearly 10,000 fans held drivers and teams hostage in '61 at the Asheville-Weaverville (NC) Speedway. True or False?

12. NASCAR drivers usually charge for autographs. True or False?

13. Jeff Gordon and Richard Petty are part-owners in this Orlando, Florida-based restaurant.

14. This company made the first race cards; they were similar to baseball cards and have become very popular since their debut in '88.

15. This organization sponsored the NASCAR Family Cruise, a fan-based cruise which featured many NASCAR drivers.

NASCAR AND THE FANS
ANSWERS

1. NASCAR Thunder
2. The NASCAR Fan Club
3. Daytona USA
4. NASCAR Cafe
5. True (www.NASCAR.com)
6. '92
7. "Most Popular Driver" award
8. Bill Elliot
9. Darrell Waltrip
10. Mattel
11. True
12. False
13. Race Rock
14. Maxx Race Cards
15. Winston Cup Racing Wives Auxiliary

CREW CHIEFS

1. Which crew chief helped Dale Earnhardt's crew take the Pit Crew Championships, four years in a row?

2. Who has been the Petty Enterprises crew chief since 1991, helping Bobby Hamilton capture his first win?

3. His call helped Jeff Gordon capture his first win in '94.

4. This former Davey Allison crew chief switched to Dale Earnhardt's team for the '97 season.

5. This brother of a legendary driver also served as his crew chief.

6. This man helped revitalize Terry Labonte's career and helped guide him to a '96 championship.

STOCK CAR TRIVIA

7. Which crew chief is the son of a legendary crew chief and helped guide Dale Jarrett to a successful '96 season?

8. He used to build stock cars for Bobby Hamilton at Nashville (TN) International Raceway.

9. He was Rusty Wallace's crew chief for the '89 Championship, later moving to Kyle Petty's team and then to the Craftsman Truck Series.

10. Who was the crew chief for Sterling Marlin's '94 and '95 Daytona 500 wins?

11. He left Dale Earnhardt's team to become part owner in Leo Jackson's #33 team.

12. This crew chief built engines that won three Daytona 500s.

13. Who used to be the crew chief for his brother-in-law, Brett Bodine?

14. He worked with Alan Kulwicki as crew chief before Kulwicki's death.

15. This Winston Cup driver wants to be a crew chief when he retires.

CREW CHIEF
ANSWERS

1. Kirk Shelmerdine, '84-'87
2. Robbie Loomis
3. Ray Evernham
4. Larry McReynolds
5. Maurice Petty
6. Gary DeHart
7. Todd Parrott
8. Gil Martin
9. Barry Dodson
10. Tony Glover
11. Andy Petree
12. Waddell Wilson
13. Donnie Richardson
14. Paul Andrews
15. Ted Musgrave

TRACKS

1. At what track did this happen? Cale Yarborough and Sam McQuagg were in a battle for the lead when the two cars touched and Cale went over the wall and landed in the parking lot.

2. The first race at this track, the World 600, took 5 hours and 34 minutes to complete.

3. The last race at this Winston Cup track took place in '96.

4. When was the last convertible race at Darlington?

5. Both qualifying races were canceled at Daytona in '68 because of what?

6. "Fireball" Roberts, Cale Yarborough and Bill Elliot are the only three drivers to score a "slam" at the Daytona 500. What is a "slam"?

7. What are the two road courses in Winston Cup competition?

8. Which track held its first night race in October '98, four months after it was scheduled?

9. Phoenix International Raceway is known as what?

10. At this track you get "the stripe," especially when you hit its famed 23 - 25 degree turns.

11. What headache powder sponsors this race at Martinsville?

12. Hosting a Winston Cup race since '69, the second yearly race at this track used to be called the "Yankee 500."

13. An old cotton field was used to create this South Carolina Winston Cup track.

14. Darrell Waltrip can claim the most consecutive wins (7) at this Tennessee track from '81-'84.

15. This track now hosts the Winston Select event each May.

STOCK CAR TRIVIA

TRACKS
ANSWERS

1. Darlington
2. Charlotte Motor Speedway
3. North Wilkesboro
4. '62 (Rebel 300)
5. Rain
6. Pole, fast qualifier and winner
7. Sears Point and Watkins Glen
8. Daytona International Speedway
9. The Jewel of the Desert
10. Darlington
11. Goody's
12. Michigan
13. Darlington
14. Bristol
15. Charlotte

ROOKIES

1. This '77 Rookie of the Year took seven years to win his first race. He's won at least one every year since.

2. This Rookie of the Year had no competition in '96.

3. This champion ran for Rookie of the Year honors versus Dale Earnhardt, Harry Gant and Joe Millikan.

4. He is the oldest driver to win Rookie of the Year.

5. This driver was a rookie when he won his first Winston Cup race in '87.

6. Who won the '79 Rookie of the Year and the '80 Winston Cup championship?

7. Who was the first Rookie of the Year?

8. Bobby Hamilton won the '91 Rookie of the Year title over what current driver?

9. Which one of these drivers was not a Rookie of the Year in the '80s: Geoff Bodine, Sterling Marlin, Rusty Wallace, Ken Schrader, Alan Kulwicki, Davey Allison, Dick Trickle or Bobby Labonte.

10. Which brothers were Rookie of the Year winners in '81 and '88, respectively?

11. Six Winston Cup Rookie of the Year titlists went on to win the Winston Cup Championship. They are Richard Petty, Dale Earnhardt, David Pearson, Rusty Wallace, Alan Kulwicki and _____.

12. The Rookie of the Year competition is sponsored by which race card company?

13. Which Rookie of the Year has a successful All-Pro career?

14. This '98 Rookie of the Year replaced Ernie Irvin in the #28 Texaco Ford.

15. Which '92 Rookie of the Year candidate now races in the truck division?

ROOKIES
ANSWERS

1. Ricky Rudd
2. Johnny Benson
3. Terry Labonte
4. Dick Trickle (48 years old)
5. Davey Allison
6. Dale Earnhardt
7. Shorty Rollins
8. Ted Musgrave
9. Bobby Labonte
10. Ron and Ken Bouchard
11. Jeff Gordon
12. Maxx Race Cards
13. Jody Ridley
14. Kenny Irwin
15. Jimmy Hensley ('92 winner)

RECORDS

1. He broke Richard Petty's string of consecutive starts (513) in April '96 at Martinsville.

2. Dale Earnhardt and Richard Petty have tied for this number of championships.

3. Which legendary car owner has a record of 609 consecutive starts?

4. Who is the winningist active driver at Daytona?

5. How many Winston Cup races were run in '64? Is that a record?

6. Which late driver has the most poles for a season?

7. From '72 to '95, this driver from Owensboro, KY had 59 poles.

8. Which driver has started the most races in his career (1,177)?

9. Which driver made the most money in one season, including championship money?

10. This driver is in the Guiness Book of World Records for the most modified wins.

11. Which active driver has won the most races from the pole?

12. Which late driver started the most consecutive races without a single win (653)?

13. This driver has the best win percentage for his career: 42 wins, 189 starts '93-'98.

14. Which driver the father of a current Busch Grand National driver won 11 races in 18 starts in '73?

15. Which driver raced more than 200 m.p.h. 15 times during his career?

RECORDS
ANSWERS

1. Terry Labonte
2. Seven
3. Bud Moore
4. Dale Earnhardt
5. 62, yes that is the highest number for a Winston Cup season
6. Bobby Isaac (20 in '69)
7. Darrell Waltrip
8. Richard Petty
9. Jeff Gordon
10. Geoffrey Bodine
11. Darrell Waltrip (24 from '72-'95)
12. J.D. McDuffie
13. Jeff Gordon, 22.2 percent
14. David Pearson
15. Cale Yarborough

SECOND GENERATION DRIVERS

Match these racing children with their parents

1. Ned Jarrett
2. Bobby Allison
3. Richard Petty
4. Arlo Andretti
5. Dale Earnhardt
6. Geoff Bodine
7. Dale Jarrett
8. Bill France
9. Ralph Earnhardt
10. Bobby Hamilton
11. Kyle Petty
12. Lee Petty
13. Rick Hendrick

a. Kelley
b. Adam
c. Kyle
d. Dale
e. Davey
f. Glenn
g. Richard
h. Ricky
i. Barry
j. Jason
k. John
l. Bobby Jr.
m. Brian

SECOND GENERATION DRIVERS
ANSWERS

1. f
2. e
3. c
4. k
5. a
6. i
7. j
8. m
9. d
10. l
11. b
12. g
13. h

SCHOOLS

1. Which college's logo was displayed on the #1 Winston Cup car?

2. Which Winston Cup driver has a degree in business management from Moravian College in Pennsylvania? (He was on the dean's list!)

3. Which Winston Cup driver has an associate's degree in mechanical engineering from the State University of New York at Alfred?

4. Which driving school is located at 15 tracks nation-wide?

5. These two people have teamed up to create the Evernham/HawleyRace Training Center in Irwindale, CA.

6. Wisconsin driver _____ received a mechanical engineering degree from the University of Wisconsin at Madison.

7. Which driver majored in mechanical engineering at the Florida Institute of Technology?

8. Jeff Gordon and Ray Evernham lectured at _____ University, making them the first NASCAR participants to lecture at an Ivy League school.

9. Which Winston Cup driver received a law degree from the University of Washington?

10. Which driver turned down a football grant from the University of Alabama?

11. This driver is a big fan of the University of Tennessee football team, often hanging out with players on the sideline during home games in Knoxville.

12. This driving school is considered the "granddaddy" of all stock car schools.

13. In '92, Richard Petty received an honorary doctorate from this college.

14. This big man at Charlotte Motor Speedway went to the University of South Carolina on a football scholarship.

15. This Kodak car owner attended Richmond Professional University before "breaking" into Winston Cup.

SCHOOLS
ANSWERS

1. University of Nebraska
2. John Andretti
3. Brett Bodine
4. The Richard Petty Driving Experience
5. Jeff Gordon Crew Chief Ray Evernham and veteran stock car driving instructor Frank Hawley
6. Alan Kulwicki
7. Joe Nemechek
8. Princeton
9. Chad Little
10. Steve Grissom
11. Sterling Marlin
12. Buck Baker's Racing School
13. Pfeiffer College
14. Humpy Wheeler
15. Larry McClure

NICKNAMES

1.	Neil Castles	a. Tiger
2.	Terry Labonte	b. Silver Fox
3.	Roy Jones	c. Ironman
4.	Fred Lorenzen	d. Jaws
5.	Jeff Gordon	e. Soapy
6.	David Pearson	f. Suitcase
7.	Edwin Keith Matthews	g. Buckshot
8.	Tom Pistone	h. Mr. Excitement
9.	Danny Myers	i. Iceman
10.	Jack Elders	j. Fearless Freddy
11.	Darrell Waltrip	k. Chocolate
12.	Jack Ingram	l. Wonder Boy
13.	Jimmy Spencer	m. Banjo

NICKNAMES
ANSWERS

1. e
2. i
3. g
4. j
5. l
6. b
7. m
8. a
9. k
10. f
11. d
12. c
13. h

EARLY RACING HISTORY

1. Automotive competition at Daytona Beach began in what year?

2. The final land speed record run on
   _____ was in '35. The
   event went to the Bonneville Salt Flats in Utah after
   that.

3. Daytona Beach was known as the birthplace of
   _____.

4. Stock car racing on the beach began in '36 and lasted until this year.

5. The original track size was _____ miles.

STOCK CAR TRIVIA

6. Bill _____ , a local mechanic, entered the beach race in '36.

7. The race stopped during WWII but resumed in what year? Motorcycle racing resumed the following year.

8. _____ , who had been promoting the beach race since '38, founded NASCAR in '48.

9. The International Sweepstakes, the first _____-mile race at the new Superspeedway, began in '59.

10. The first winner of the International Sweepstakes event was _____, but three days later Lee Petty was named the winner (by just two feet).

11. The first "new car" race was held at this track in '49.

STOCK CAR TRIVIA

12. Darlington was built in the late '40s, and in '50 the first _____ took place.

13. What year did Grand National drivers go on strike?

14. During WWII, _____ built sub chasers.

15. The National Stock Car Racing Association, NASCRA, was the first suggestion for a name, but a small group in Georgia already had the name; therefore, driver-mechanic Red Vogt suggested the National Association For Stock Car Automobile Racing, NASCAR. True or False?

EARLY RACING HISTORY
ANSWERS

1. '03
2. Daytona Beach
3. Speed
4. '58
5. 3.2
6. France
7. 1946
8. Bill France Sr.
9. 500
10. Johnny Beauchamp
11. Charlotte Motor Speedway
12. Southern 500
13. '69
14. Bill France Sr.
15. True

BUSCH GRAND NATIONAL

1. This son of a Winston Cup champ took his first BGN championship in '98.

2. Name the former BGN Rookie who was later seriously injured during his rookie cup year.

3. Which BGN driver competed in the inaugural race in Japan in '96?

4. Which '91 BGN Rookie of the Year went on to take a Winston Cup championship?

5. Only three drivers have been the BGN champ twice. Who are they?

6. Only two BGN Rookies have won the championship. Name them.

7. At Rockingham, who won his last NASCAR and first BGN series race?

8. No BGN champion has ever won a Winston Cup championship. True or False?

9. Jimmy Spencer was a BGN regular in '88 and again in what year?

10. Who won the first BGN event in '82?

11. What was BGN initially called?

12. This Gadsen, AL native was 22 years old when he won the All-Pro series title. He took the BGN title at 30 years of age.

13. Which Winston Cup driver is extremely consistent in a BGN car?

14. Owensboro, KY has produced its share of top drivers, among them this '95 BGN champion.

15. This father and son raced against each other for the first time during an exhibition race in Japan in '98.

BUSCH GRAND NATIONAL
ANSWERS

1. Dale Earnhardt Jr.
2. Steve Park
3. David Green
4. Jeff Gordon
5. Larry Pearson, Jack Ingram, Sam Arnd
6. Joe Nemechek and Johnny Benson
7. David Pearson
8. True
9. '92
10. Dale Earnhardt
11. NASCAR Budweiser Late Model Sportsman Division
12. Steve Grissom
13. Mark Martin
14. David Green
15. Dale Earnhardt and Dale Earnhardt Jr.

SPONSORS

1. What soft drink sponsor in the movie "Days of Thunder" became an actual Winston Cup sponsor?

2. What political campaign "sponsored" the car of Robbie Faggart as he attempted to qualify for the '96 Southern 500?

3. Which laundry detergent company was one of the first non-automotive-related sponsors in Winston Cup?

4. Which wrestling organization sponsored the #29 Busch Grand National car?

5. Scooby Doo and Fred Flintstone were part of whose sponsorship of the #29 Winston Cup car?

6. What official film of NASCAR also sponsors a car?

7. No matter what the type of beer—Lite, Genuine Draft—Rusty Wallace's main sponsor stays the same. What is it?

8. The sales of Goody's Headache Powders almost doubled once they became involved in stock car racing. True or False?

9. Which manufacturer pulled out of Busch Grand National/Winston Cup racing in the '70s and stayed out until '81?

10. Which sports drink company sponsored Darrell Waltrip?

11. After legislation regulating tobacco advertising, the sponsor of the #23 car changed from Joe Camel to what?

12. The Mechanic of the Race award is sponsored by what auto parts company?

13. This fuel company lent Bill France Sr. the fuel to start the NASCAR races.

14. The main sponsor for Winston Cup racing is what tobacco company?

15. What driver changed his color and sponsor for the inaugural race at Suzuka City in Japan?

STOCK CAR TRIVIA

SPONSORS
ANSWERS

1. Mello Yellow
2. Dole/Kemp '96
3. Tide
4. World Championship Wrestling (WCW)
5. Cartoon Network
6. Kodak
7. Miller
8. True
9. Ford
10. Gatorade
11. No Bull
12. Western Auto
13. Unocal
14. R.J. Reynolds
15. Earnhardt (to A.C. Delco)

BUD SHOOTOUT

1. The Bud Shootout was called what?

2. The Bud Shootout is sponsored by what company?

3. Where is the race run?

4. To qualify for the Shootout, a driver must have won a pole for a race the prior year or win the coin toss at the end of the season. True or False?

5. This driver won the first Bud Shootout in '79.

6. Dale Earnhardt won the Bud Shootout four times in the same year he won the championship. What other driver did the same ('81)?

STOCK CAR TRIVIA

7. This Pittsboro, IN driver won the Bud Shootout the first time he ran it.

8. What year did the race begin?

9. What driver has won more Shootouts than any other?

10. This driver won the 9th race in '84 with car #9. Name him.

11. Which two drivers have won the race in back-to-back years.

12. Which driver needed directions to Victory Lane after winning the Bud Shootout in '98?

13. The Bud Shootout is run the week prior to what race?

14. How many laps does the actual Bud Shootout consist of?

15. The following have won the Shootout but not the Winston Cup Championship: Buddy Baker, Neil Bonnett, Kenny Schrader and _____.

BUD SHOOTOUT
ANSWERS

1. Busch Clash
2. Anheuser-Busch
3. Daytona International Speedway
4. False, the coin toss is not a part of the determination. The winner of the Bud Shoot qualifying race also gets to take part in the Shootout.
5. Buddy Baker
6. Darrell Waltrip
7. Jeff Gordon
8. '79
9. Dale Earnhardt
10. Bill Elliott
11. Neil Bonnett ('83, '84) and Ken Schrader ('89, '90)
12. Rusty Wallace
13. Daytona 500
14. 25
15. Geoff Bodine

STOCK CAR TRIVIA

TRUE OR FALSE

Answer true or false to each of the following:

1. Curtis Turner was suspended by NASCAR in '61 for trying to unionize the drivers.

2. Bobby Hamilton won two poles in '96 and therefore was in the Busch Clash.

3. The speedway stocks (on the stock market) are not offered to the general public.

4. When R.J. Reynolds initially put up the money for the first Winston million, they didn't think anyone would win. Elliott surprised them.

STOCK CAR TRIVIA

5. Dale Jarrett drove his first professional race at Hickory, NC in '77 in a car built by Andy Petree and Jimmy Newsome.

6. The National Motorsports Press Association's Hall of Fame is located at Rockingham.

7. Jim Boy and Bucky are a popular syndicated radio duo who love racing.

8. Atlanta Motor Speedway is a tri-oval.

9. NASCAR opened an office in Washington, D.C., in '96.

10. Speed Buggy joined forces with ESPN and NASCAR for a promotional campaign.

11. The Joe Weatherly Museum is at Darlington Raceway.

12. Richard Petty was the first inductee of the North Carolina Auto Racing Hall of Fame.

13. Harry Hogge built Rick Hendrick's first cars and also served as the team's crew chief.

14. Ken Schrader's first Winston Cup ride was for the late Elmo Langley.

15. Eli Gold also announces football games for Auburn University.

TRUE OR FALSE
ANSWERS

1. True
2. False (Petty Enterprises does not run the Busch Beer logo on the #43 car, so Hamilton and the team are not eligible for the Clash.)
3. False
4. True
5. True
6. False (Darlington)
7. False (John Boy and Billy are the duo, based out of Charlotte.)
8. False (It is a quad-oval)
9. False (New York City)
10. False (It was Speed Racer.)
11. True
12. True
13. False (Harry Hyde was his name.)
14. True
15. False (University of Alabama)

HOBBIES

1. What driver from Chesapeake, VA enjoys listening to Elton John music?

2. This third-generation driver loves riding his Harley-Davidson ™ motorcycle.

3. What former Daytona 500 winner is an excellent golfer?

4. This seven-time Winston Cup champion driver loves to fish and hunt.

5. He's flown in a race car (he holds the fastest race speed record) and loves to fly in a plane.

6. This driver loves video games.

7. This two-time Daytona 500 winner loves to collect Civil War relics.

8. This Roush driver is a devout body builder.

9. This Wisconsin driver loves to restore vintage vehicles.

10. This Missouri native loves collecting old cars and trucks.

11. This driver loves roller skating.

12. Karaoke is the favorite hobby of this Alabama driver.

13. This driver, the youngest of three brothers, loves the St. Louis Cardinals.

STOCK CAR TRIVIA

14. His oldest brother loves the National Hot Rod Association.
15. This driver "dabbles" with computers and remote control cars.

HOBBIES
ANSWERS

1. Ricky Rudd
2. Kyle Petty
3. Derrike Cope
4. Dale Earnhardt
5. Bill Elliott
6. Jeff Gordon
7. Sterling Marlin
8. Mark Martin
9. Ted Musgrave
10. Ken Schrader
11. Morgan Shepherd
12. Hut Stricklin
13. Kenny Wallace
14. Rusty Wallace
15. Bobby Labonte

COOL FACTS

1. Who started his first Winston Cup race as a 17-year-old high school student in '82?

2. His grandfather built cars for the late country singer Marty Robbins.

3. He is A.J. Foyt's godson.

4. Richard Petty is a staunch Republican. He ran for what North Carolina office in '96?

5. Bobby Hamilton won at Phoenix International Raceway, a track where he first caught Winston Cup's eye as a driver in what?

6. He and his family have a "dirt track" next to the family's auto parts business. Winston Cup drivers "race" there during Pocono weekends.

7. He traded $300 worth of lumber for a motor for his son Dale's first race car.

8. What track's grandstands are named for legendary stock car racers?

9. In '94, which driver raced in the Indianapolis 500 and the Coca Cola 600 on the same day?

10. This driver and the Penske Racing team worked with Rockwell Space Systems Division in '96.

11. The _____ season is where drivers, teams and sponsors switch around.

12. In the '38 _____ beach race, lap winners
    were offered a bottle of rum, $2.50 credit at a local
    men's store, a box of fancy Hav-A-Tampa cigars, a
    case of Pennzoil oil and a $25 credit toward the pur-
    chase of a car at a local used automobile lot.

13. Over 3 million bricks were used whan this track was
    originally laid.

14. What racing publication as known as the bible of
    stock car racing?

15. There are just six drivers who have made $1 million
    in two series (Busch Grand National and Winston
    Cup). They are Bobby Labonte, Robert Pressley,
    Kenny Wallace, Steve Grissom, Dale Jarrett and

    _____.

COOL FACTS
ANSWER

1. Bobby Hillen
2. Bobby Hamilton
3. John Andretti
4. Secretary of State
5. Days of Thunder
6. Jimmy Spencer
7. Ned Jarrett
8. Bristol Motor Speedway
9. John Andretti
10. Rusty Wallace
11. Silly
12. Daytona
13. Indianapolis Motor Speedway
14. Winston Cup Scene
15. Mark Martin

CAR OWNERS

1. Which two team owners have won back-to-back championships with different drivers?

2. Which car owner has five Winston Cup teams?

3. The _____ Brothers have been together for more than 800 races over 45 years.

4. Dale Earnhardt has raced for how many Winston Cup car owners since '75?

5. Junior Johnson left racing as car owner at the end of the _____ season.

6. Who moved his race team from Hueytown to Charlotte in '96?

7. Chad Little's BGN car owner was which Washington Redskin football player?

8. This car owner won four straight Winston Cup championships.

9. He bought the team from the Alan Kulwicki estate.

10. This car owner has earned more prize money than any other in the history of Winston Cup.

11. Which car owner was formerly an NFL coach?

12. Which Winston Cup driver also has owned his car for over 30 years?

13. This five-team car owner is a former drag racer.

14. This team owner was one of the original members of the Mach One team owned by Burt Reynolds and Hal Needham during Harry Gant's Skoal Bandit career.

15. This driver brought Richard Petty his first win as a car owner.

CAR OWNERS
ANSWERS

1. Carl Kiekhaefer and Rick Hendrick
2. Jack Rousch (Johnny Benson, Jeff Burton, Kevin LePage, Chad Little and Mark Martin)
3. Wood
4. Nine
5. '95
6. Bobby Allison
7. Mark Rypien
8. Rick Hendrick, ('95 to '98)
9. Geoff Bodine
10. Rick Hendrick
11. Joe Gibbs
12. Dave Marcis
13. Jack Roush
14. Travis Carter
15. Bobby Hamilton

MONEY AND OTHER IMPORTANT NUMBERS

1. If the Winston Million had been in effect, two other drivers would have won the money. Name them.

2. Richard Petty Enterprises and STP celebrated ___ years together in '96 with commemorative colors on the #43 car.

3. Talladega cost $4 million to build in '69, but this track cost $200 million to build in '97.

4. NASCAR sanctions races in how many states?

5. First place in a race garners the driver how many points?

6. In a 44-car field, last place gets this number of points.

7. Leading a lap gives a driver _____ extra points.

8. This driver is the only one to win 10 races or more in three consecutive years.

9. A track is a "short track" if it is less than _____.

10. The '84 Winston 500 at _____ saw 75 lead changes in 188 laps.

11. This Winston Cup driver has won the most money (more than $28 million at the end of the '96 season).

12. Jeff Gordon won more than _____ in '98 (total earnings).

13. This driver led the most laps at the '61 Daytona 500 but didn't win.

14. This driver is second to Richard Petty in wins and poles.

15. This Busch Grand National driver has won the most money in that division (more than $1.8 million)

MONEY AND OTHER IMPORTANT NUMBERS
ANSWERS

1. Lee Roy Yarborough, ('69) and David Pearson ('76)
2. 25th
3. Las Vegas Motor Speedway
4. 39
5. 175
6. 31
7. 5
8. Jeff Gordon
9. 1 mile
10. Talladega
11. Dale Earnhardt
12. $9 million
13. Fireball Roberts
14. David Pearson
15. Tommy Houston

FIRST AND LAST

1. Which driver won the first Brickyard 400?

2. He won his first race at New Hampshire after surviving a near fatal crash at Michigan in '94.

3. She was the first woman driver in a Winston Cup race in the modern era. Name her.

4. On which track did Jeremy Mayfield win his first race? It was also the first time a first-time winner won there.

5. There were no first time Winston Cup winners in '72. True or False?

6. Who was the first to win the Daytona 500 and the Brickyard 400 in the same year?

7. Who won the '96 exhibition at Suzuka City, Japan?

8. Which NASCAR driver was the first to compete in Japan?

9. The first drivers inducted into the National Motorsports Press Association Stock Car Hall of Fame was Joe Weatherly, Herb Thomas, mechanic Paul McDuffie and _____.

10. Who won the last Winston Cup race at North Wilkesboro?

11. Richard Petty made his first million in what year?

12. It took 74 hours to determine the first winner of the '59 _____.

13. The first Daytona 500 was run caution free. True or False?

14. The first NMPS Driver of the Year was which Yarborough?

15. Which late Winston Cup driver won his first race in '87?

FIRST AND LAST
ANSWERS

1. Jeff Gordon
2. Ernie Irvan
3. Janet Guthrie
4. Pocono
5. True
6. Dale Jarrett
7. Rusty Wallace
8. Tiny Lund ('70 stock car race)
9. "Fireball" Roberts
10. Jeff Gordon
11. '71
12. Daytona 500
13. True
14. Lee Roy
15. Davey Allison

WRECKS

1. Which Winston Cup driver "flew" out of the track at Talladega? He was later nicknamed "Air."

2. Three drivers' lives were taken in on-track wrecks in '64. They were Joe Weatherly, Fireball Roberts and

   _____.

3. Two wrecks at Talladega in April '96 were dramatic, yet the drivers walked away. Name the main drivers involved.

4. Dale Earnhardt has seen two bad wrecks in his 18-year career, one in _____ and one in '96.

5. This driver flipped at Talladega and which other track in '93?

6. This driver saw his car virtually destroyed at Talladega in July '95.

7. This BGN driver was fortunate to only have burned his hands and neck in a Homestead, FL explosion during a last chance race in '96.

8. After this wreck during the '79 Daytona 500, these three drivers stepped out of their car on the backstretch and proceeded to fight it out.

9. Sadly, drivers have been killed as a result of the _____ qualifying races for the Daytona 500. They were: Talmadge Prince ('70), Friday Hassler ('72), Ricky Knotts ('80) and Bruce Jacobi ('87).

10. Michael Waltrip's totally destroyed car, involved in a wreck at _____, sits in the museum at Talladega.

11. This track has been the scene of more bizarre incidents than any other on the circuit.

12. Which racing legend saw his career end early due to a wreck at Pocono in '88?

13. This champion miraculously survived a tumbling roll down the front straight-away at Daytona.

14. This driver captured a heart-stopping win over Richard Petty on the final lap after the two crashed in one of the most famous Daytona 500 races ever.

15. Cole Trickle t-boned what driver in "Days of Thunder"?

STOCK CAR TRIVIA

WRECKS
ANSWERS

1. Jimmy Horton
2. Jimmy Pardue
3. Ricky Craven and Bill Elliot
4. '79
5. Daytona
6. Ken Schrader
7. Michael Laughlin
8. Donnie Allison, Bobby Allison and Cale Yarborough
9. Twin 125
10. Bristol
11. Talladega
12. Bobby Allison
13. Daytona
14. David Pearson
15. Rowdy Barnes

CRAFTSMAN TRUCK SERIES

1. Who is the first female driver in a truck race?

2. The first black man to race a truck is
   _____.

3. The series' first champion moved to Winston Cup in '97. Name him.

4. These former truck drivers were Winston Cup Rookies of the Year.

5. Ron Hornaday won the '98 truck championhip by _____ points over Jack Sprague.

6. The trucks moved to Orlando in '97 to race at this "magical" Speedway.

STOCK CAR TRIVIA

7. This man was the first winner of the series' Rookie of the Year award.

8. What corporation owns the truck driven by Ron Hornaday Jr.?

9. The series is sponsored by this subsidiary of Sears.

10. The trucks were previewed in this series on TNN prior to their first season?

11. The first winner of a truck race was _____.

12. This retired Winston Cup driver resurfaced as a truck driver.

13. This '92 Winston Cup Rookie of the Year now drives a truck.

STOCK CAR TRIVIA

14. This female truck driver's truck was sponsored by a bra company. Name her and the company.

15. The youngest truck competitor was just 16 when he raced for Bobby Hamilton in Nashville, TN '96 event. Name the young Hamilton protegé.

CRAFTSMAN TRUCK SERIES
ANSWERS

1. Tammy Jo Kirk
2. Felix Giles
3. Mike Skinner
4. Mike Skinner, Kenny Irwin
5. Three
6. Walt Disney World
7. Bryan Reffner
8. Dale Earnhardt, Inc.
9. Craftsman
10. Winter Heat
11. Mike Skinner
12. Harry Gant
13. Jimmy Hensley
14. Tammy Jo Kirk, Lovable
15. Casey Atwood

DRIVERS

1. Which driver was fired by Chrysler when he won a race driving a Chevrolet?

2. This Bodine first drove for Rick Hendrick.

3. This Winston Cup driver created bobsleds for the Olympic team.

4. What former driver for Bobby Allison Motorsports was the '83 Late Model Sportsman Champion?

5. These two drivers shared the '86 Driver of the Year award.

6. His '88 championship made him the first Ford driver to win the title since David Pearson.

7. He was the youngest title holder since Bill Rexford won in '50.

8. Who raced go-karts, CART, USAC, Le Mans, Indy, NHRA and more before moving to Winston Cup?

9. This driver won the '93 Busch Grand National championship.

10. His big break came in the Superstar Showdown at Nashville in '88. He beat Bill Elliot, Darrell Waltrip and others.

11. Who was 22 when he won the Talladega 500?

12. Despite his near-fatal wreck, this driver won the '94 True Value Hard Charger Award. He had competed in just 20 events that year.

13. Who is nearly a scratch handicap golfer?

14. His first career win came in the '95 Coca Cola 600.

15. At Bristol in '96, he clashed with Dale Earnhardt and came across the line backwards. His was one of the few cars in Victory Lane that was actually torn up!

DRIVERS
ANSWERS

1. Bobby Allison
2. Brett
3. Geoff Bodine (the Bo-Dyn sled)
4. Derrike Cope
5. Dale Earnhardt and Tim Richmond
6. Bill Elliot
7. Jeff Gordon
8. John Andretti
9. Steve Grissom
10. Bobby Hamilton
11. Bobby Hillen
12. Ernie Irvan
13. Dale Jarrett
14. Bobby Labonte
15. Terry Labonte

MORE DRIVERS

1. This driver is known for his black leather hard-soled shoes he wears during the races.

2. This Tennessee native made his Winston Cup debut after his dad broke his shoulder in a '76 crash.

3. This driver once showed up to a race in a three-piece suit, after being told that he needed to "clean up his act."

4. Who won the pole for the first Brickyard 400?

5. This young driver grew up in Owensboro, KY idolizing Darrell Waltrip.

6. This driver won eight of 12 races at Bristol.

STOCK CAR TRIVIA

7. This '90 BGN Rookie of the Year was the champion in '92.

8. Who was the first third-generation driver to win a cup race?

9. President Ronald Regan and Vice President George Bush gave Richard Petty what award?

10. _____ was mentioned by Bruce Springsteen in a song.

11. He and his wife Patty Moise both drive stock cars. Who is he?

12. This driver was the World Karting Champion, taking the title in Le Mans, France in '78.

13. Which driver filled in for Ernie Irvan after Irvan's crash in '94?

14. Name the Penske driver who won the '91 IROC.

15. This driver has won at least one race each year since '83.

MORE DRIVERS
ANSWERS

1. Dave Marcis
2. Sterling Marlin
3. Curtis Turner
4. Rick Mast
5. Jeremy Mayfield
6. Cale Yarbrough
7. Joe Nemechek
8. Kyle Petty
9. Freedom Award
10. Junior Johnson
11. Elton Sawyer
12. Lake Speed
13. Kenny Wallace
14. Rusty Wallace
15. Ricky Rudd

TRUE OR FALSE, PART TWO

1. An Edsel ran in the first Daytona 500.

2. Both Derrick Cope and Jeff Gordon married former Miss Winstons.

3. ARCA is sanctioned by NASCAR.

4. A Chevy truck was the pace car for the second Brickyard 400.

5. Mario Andretti drove for Richard Petty in '95.

6. Jeff Gordon won his first pole at Rockingham.

7. Harry Gant's Farewell Tour was in '92.

8. John Andretti is the only person to have wrecked cars in both Winston Cup and Indy car divisions at Indianapolis.

9. The Alan Kulwicki Park is located in Bristol, TN.

10. "Tie Rod" is the official mascot of Charlotte Motor Speedway.

11. Randolph Scott was the first black NASCAR driver.

12. Junior Johnson spent a year in jail for bootlegging.

13. Motor Racing Outreach is the ministerial organization of NASCAR.

14. Brooks & Dunn and Rusty Wallace wrote the song "Sunday Money" together. The song was featured on a later album.

15. A brick from the Brickyard was laid at Walt Disney World Speedway.

TRUE OR FALSE, PART TWO
ANSWERS

1. True
2. True
3. False
4. True
5. False, it was John Andretti.
6. False, it was at Charlotte.
7. False, it was in '94.
8. True
9. False, it is in Greenfield, Wisconsin.
10. False, it's name is "Lug Nut."
11. False, his name was Wendall Scott.
12. True
13. True
14. False, Dale Earnhardt was the driver, and the album was the Dale Earnhardt Winston Cup Collection.
15. True

PART-TIME JOBS

1. This Goody's Dash series driver is also a doctor.

2. What current star was a welder on the Charlotte Motor Speedway grandstands when he first moved to Charlotte?

3. This driver owns a Honda dealership in Franklin, TN.

4. Which driver once had a country music "career" as well as a driving career?

5. This driver worked on his older brother Benny's Winston Cup team before getting his own rides.

6. This driver has raced just about everything. He still finds time to co own auto parts stores.

7. He is a former volunteer fireman.

8. Which driver enjoys working as a TV announcer when he's not driving or rooting for the St. Louis Cardinals?

9. This driver could take an automobile apart and put it back together when he was 11.

10. This driver once drove a bread truck, but it wasn't his job. He used it as a tow vehicle for his race cars.

11. Who was a professional baseball prospect (as a catcher) before a knee injury ended his career?

12. This independent driver would like to run a fishing resort or restaurant when his driving days are through.

STOCK CAR TRIVIA

13. Who teamed up with Cleveland Cavaliers center Brad Daugherty to form his BGN team?

14. This country music artist's part-time career was Grand National racing. He competed in 43 races during his career.

15. This driver (later car owner) ran moonshine for his family when he first broke into racing.

PART-TIME JOBS
ANSWERS

1. Dr. Thomas "Doc" Brewer
2. Ernie Irvan
3. Darrell Waltrip
4. Kyle Petty
5. Phil Parsons
6. John Andretti
7. Geoff Bodine
8. Kenny Wallace
9. Morgan Shepherd
10. Rusty Wallace
11. Derrike Cope
12. Dave Marcis
13. Robert Pressley
14. Marty Robbins
15. Junior Johnson

THE LEGENDS

1. Which legendary car owner and crew chief won the '62 and '63 Winston Cup championships with Joe Weatherly as driver?

2. After this driver won the '56 championship, he took over the ownership of his team. He won again. Now there's a driving school in his name.

3. This Golden Boy of the '60s was the first driver to top $100,000 in a single season. He was also the first to score a Grand Slam with victories on the original five super-speedways.

4. This father of a current Winston Cup driver now owns a tobacco farm near Columbia, TN.

5. Which Grand National driver is a former movie stuntman, working on films such as "Speedway" and "Six Pack"?

STOCK CAR TRIVIA

6. This younger brother of The King is a master engine builder.

7. Who was the first Miss Winston, starting in the '71 season?

8. Second only to Richard Petty on the all-time list of wins and poles, this former driver set innumerable records during his 26-year career.

9. This late driver was Winston Cup's pace car driver when he died during a tour of the Suzuka City Circuitland track in '96.

10. Who won the '75 Daytona 500 and now works as a color commentator on television coverage of Winston Cup races?

11. This former flagman used to work in the same position at Nashville Speedway. He worked with drivers such as Darrell Waltrip, Jimmy Means and Sterling Marlin.

12. This legendary driver is one of the original members of the Alabama Gang.

13. Which late flagman had the duty for more than 25 years before retiring after the May 6 Talladega race in '90?

14. Born in Chicago, this driver went on to win five poles and two races . He's known for his innovations, including the NASCAR screw jack, first used in '55.

15. This driver won the '61 and '65 championships while gaining a name for himself as one of the most personable drivers on the circuit. Today, one son has joined him in the television world while the other son races.

THE LEGENDS
ANSWERS

1. Walter "Bud" Moore
2. Buck Baker
3. Fred Lorenzen
4. Clifton "Coo Coo" Marlin
5. Neil "Soapy" Castles
6. Maurice Petty
7. Marilyn Green
8. David Pearson
9. Elmo Langley
10. Benny Parsons
11. Doyle Ford
12. Bobby Allison
13. Harold Kinder
14. "Tiger" Tom Pistone
15. Ned Jarrett

Premium gift books from PREMIUM PRESS AMERICA include:

I'LL BE DOGGONE
CATS OUT OF THE BAG

STOCK CAR TRIVIA
STOCK CAR GAMES
STOCK CAR DRIVERS & TRACKS
STOCK CAR LEGENDS

GREAT AMERICAN CIVIL WAR
GREAT AMERICAN COUNTRY MUSIC
GREAT AMERICAN GOLF
GREAT AMERICAN STOCK CAR RACING

ANGELS EVERYWHERE
MILLENNIUM MADNESS

ABSOLUTELY ALABAMA
AMAZING ARKANSAS
FABULOUS FLORIDA
GORGEOUS GEORGIA
SENSATIONAL SOUTH CAROLINA
TERRIFIC TENNESSEE
VINTAGE VIRGINIA

TITANIC TRIVIA
LEONARDO—TEEN IDOL

BILL DANCES FISHING TIPS
DREAM CATCHERS
THE REDNECK GUIDE TO WINE
    SNOBBERY

PREMIUM PRESS AMERICA routinely updates existing titles and frequently adds new topics to its growing line of premium gift books. Books are distributed though gift and specialty shops, and bookstores nationwide. If, for any reason, books are not available in your area, please contact the local distributor listed above or contact the Publisher direct by calling 1-800-891-7323. To see our complete backlist and current books, you can visit our website at www.premiumpress.com. Thank you.

Great Reading.   Premium Gifts.